I Wonder

Answers to Religious Questions Children Ask

I Wonder

Answers to Religious Questions Children Ask
By Allan Hart Jahsmann
Illustrated by Dick Cosper
Designed by Number Ten, Inc.

To my editor, Pat McKissack, and to my secretary,
Phillis Meeks. Their personal interest in the book
kept me at it and helped make it what it is.

I Wonder
Copyright © 1979 by Concordia Publishing House
3558 South Jefferson Avenue, St. Louis, MO 63118

Library of Congress Catalog Card Number:
ISBN 0-570-03473-6

Printed in the United States of America

Scripture quotations in this book are from *The Holy Bible for Children* (HBFC),
copyrighted © 1977 by Concordia Publishing House, and from *The Good News
Bible,* copyrighted © TEV, 1966, 1971, 1976 by the American Bible Society. Both
were used by permission.

Contents

Questions

About God

How can I be sure there's a God?

What's God like?

How old is God?

How can God be everywhere at the same time?

Why do we call God "our Father"?

In a book of children's letters to God a girl wrote, "Dear God: Are boys better than girls? I know You are one, but try to be fair."

What is the Holy Spirit?

Does the Holy Ghost look like Casper—white sheet and all?

One of the Ten Commandments says, "You should have no other gods before Me." What does that mean?

Is it true that God helps those who help themselves?

If God can do anything, why didn't He make my mother well?

If God has the power to turn bad things into something good, why doesn't He?

Why does God let bad things happen?

Where was God when my friend was hit by a car?

My teacher said God lives in people. Does God live in me?

People say that God loves everybody, but does He love killers too?

If I do something very bad, will God punish me?

Why doesn't God get rid of all bad people and let only the good people live?

If God loves and protects us, why doesn't He warn us when an earthquake is going to happen, or a flood, or a tornado?

Does God ever get angry and punish people?

I'm afraid of thunder storms. Is God angry when it storms?

The grace of God—what's that?

Is God against people going to other planets?

Can I be sure God will help me when I need help?

Why did God create mice and roaches and fleas and things like that?

About Jesus

Was Jesus God?

Why is Jesus called the Savior?

What does it mean to believe in Jesus?

Was Jesus really born on the 25th day of December?

Was Jesus a normal kid?

Did Jesus have any brothers and sisters?

Did Jesus have any children?

Did Jesus ever have any fun?

Did Jesus say He was God?

What did Jesus mean when He said, "Whoever has seen Me has seen the Father?"

Why is Jesus sometimes called Lord?

If Jesus is God, did He pray to Himself?

Why was Jesus crucified?

If Jesus had the power to save Himself, why didn't He?

What were the last words Jesus said on the cross?

Why did Jesus wash the feet of His disciples?

Will Jesus come again? Some say He's here now.

What is "the world to come"? I thought there was only one world.

What happened to all the people who lived before Jesus came and died for them?

About Sin and Forgiveness

What is sin?

Is there such a thing as a little sin?

Is it a sin to swear if I don't take God's name in vain?

My friend says it's against the law to eat pork. We ate pork chops last night. Did we do something wrong?

My parents are divorced. Are they sinners?

Are people who work on Sunday committing a sin?

When I say "gosh" and "gee" and "golly," are those bad words? My grandma says they are.

Why do people steal and kill?

Is it all right to get angry?

Why doesn't God make people be good instead of letting them do bad things?

In Bible days some men had lots of wives. If it's wrong now, why wasn't it wrong *then*?

What does covet mean?

What makes people jealous?

What's the difference between a soldier killing people in war and just plain murder?

I love to talk. Is talking too much a sin?

Is there any sure way to keep from sinning?

My father sins. Will he go to heaven?

About Being a Christian

Am I a Christian?

What can *I* do for God?

How can I know what God wants me to do?

When the Bible tells me to love my neighbor, what does that mean?

I know the Bible tells us to love everybody. But can I be a Christian and not LIKE everybody?

How can I love someone who hates me?

What's a talent and who has it?

How can I know what's right and fair?

Why is it better to give than to receive?

Do I have to go to church to be a Christian?

What will make me happy?

How do people become saints?

Is it true that when I *think* bad things, it's as bad as *doing* bad things?

I stole a comic book in a drug store once. No one saw me and I'm sorry I did it. But it still bothers me. Why?

Is cleanliness really next to godliness?

Why did God make me the way I am?

What's an atheist?

I read a book about Christian presidents and Thomas Jefferson wasn't included. They said he was a deist. What's that?

How can I be sure I'm not believing a false prophet?

What does it mean to keep the faith?

My teacher told me to let my conscience be my guide. What's my conscience?

Is it all right to fail?

If my parents are Christians, how come they often get angry at me?

Why should we share what God gives to us? Doesn't He want us to have what He gives?

What does it mean to tithe?

About Churches and Worship

What does the word "denomination" mean?

Why are there so many different kinds of churches?

Will something bad happen to me if I miss church?

Is it all right to have friends who don't go to church?

Do I have to dress up to go to church?

Why do some people go to church on Saturdays and some on Sundays?

Is it wrong to laugh in church?

Why don't some people sing in the church service?

What is a seminary?

Who is a "man of the cloth"?

What does a minister do all week?

Are only pastors and priests allowed to preach in a church?

Why do churches baptize people?

Can children be baptized without their parents' permission?

In some churches you can't take Communion until you're confirmed. Why is that?

What is confirmation?

What is the Apostles' Creed?

What's the communion of saints?

What does the word evangelical mean?

Why do Roman Catholics call their church service a "mass"?

Is it okay for me to go to church if I have no money to put in the offering?

Is it true that the more I give to the church, the more I'll get from God?

Why is Easter on a different day every year?

What is Lent?

Why is the first day of Lent called "Ash Wednesday"?

About the Bible and Prayer

What's the Bible?

Why is the Bible called God's book?

Who put the 66 Bible books together?

Why is the Bible divided into two parts?

What's a testament?

God talked to Moses and Abraham and other people in the Bible. Does He talk to people today?

What's the Gospel?

What's an epistle?

What is a prophet?

What is a proverb?

What is a psalm?

Why is the Bible sometimes called the King James Version?

Which is the best version to use?

Is it wrong to burn a Bible?

The Bible says I should be happy all the time. How is that possible?

Why should I pray?

What good does it do to pray?

Do I have to kneel to pray?

Is it necessary to pray every day?

Why do people say "Amen" at the end of prayers? Do I have to?

What should I pray for?

Why doesn't God answer all prayers?

The Lord's Prayer is said in different ways. What way is right?

At the end of the Lord's Prayer people say, "For Thine is the Kingdom and the power and the glory." What is the Kingdom?

About Angels and Devils and Heaven and Hell

What's an angel?

Do angels have wings?

Are all angels white?

Are angels male or female?

Is there such a thing as a guardian angel?

Are there really angels all around us?

What are cherubs?

Is there really a devil?

Does the devil look like the pictures I've seen of him?

What does it mean when people say, "The devil made me do it"?

If God is more powerful than the devil, why does He let him exist?

Are there really people who worship the devil?

Is it possible to sell your soul to the devil?

My mother is going to have a baby. She said that the baby will be a gift from heaven. What does that mean?

Where is heaven?

What's heaven like?

Are there really golden gates in heaven?

What are the heavenly mansions?

Will I go to heaven if I'm good?

How can I be sure to get into heaven?

When I die, will I become a ghost?

Why does God let people die?

Do people know each other in heaven?

Do dogs and cats go to heaven?

Can people come back to life after they die?

My minister said, "Hell is where God isn't." What does that mean?

Is it possible to enter heaven without dying?

About This and That

Why do some people say, "God bless you," when I sneeze?

Will I live to be a grandmother?

What is the Passover?

Why do Jews celebrate New Year's Day in the fall?

Why do people have to starve if God could feed them?

What's a miracle?

Do miracles still happen?

What keeps the moon from falling?

Is it all right to give your body to science or parts (transplants) to other people?

Is it all right to burn a dead body?

Why do people live in families?

Is it all right for girls to look like boys?

Why do countries fight each other?

What makes clouds and rain and snow?

Can people really see into the future?

Is gambling a sin?

Why are church doors often painted red?

In social studies we learned that there is supposed to be a separation of church and state in our country. What does that mean?

My sister fasts once a week in order to lose weight. She says fasting is commanded in the Bible. Is this true?

All God's children are supposed to be free. How free can I be?

What do people mean when they say, "The peace of the Lord," to each other in a church service?

About God

How can I be sure there's a God?

You can get to know *about* God in many ways. The Bible tells a great many things about God. But only when you receive His Spirit and fall in love with God will you be sure there is a God who is wonderful and good.

What's God like?

The disciple of Jesus called John wrote, "No one has ever seen God. The only Son, who is the same as God and is at the Father's side, He has made Him known" (John 1:18 TEV). And in one of his letters John wrote again, "No one has ever seen God." But then he added, "When we love one another, God lives in us" (John 4:12 HBFC). So you can learn to know what God is like when you treat people in kind and loving ways, as Jesus did.

How old is God?

There never was a time when God didn't exist. The very first words of the Bible say, "In the beginning God . . ." And there'll never be a time when God is not around. He is eternal. That's a good thing to remember.

How can God be everywhere at the same time?

God is a spirit, and a spirit can be in many places at the same time. In one of the psalms in the Bible King David said to God, "If I went up to heaven, You would be there; if I lay down in the world of the dead, You would be there. If I flew away beyond the east or lived in the farthest place in the west, You would be there to lead me; You would be there to help me." (Psalm 139:8-10 TEV)

Why do we call God "our Father"?

Jesus called God His Father in heaven. God is not like some fathers, but God was a loving, caring father to Him. And Jesus taught us to call God our heavenly Father. He wanted us to think of God's love and care for us too.

In a book of children's letters to God a girl wrote:
"Dear God: Are boys better than girls? I know You are one, but try to be fair."

This girl thought God was a male rather than a female person. Most other people do too. God's been pictured as an old man, and Jesus taught us to call Him, "our Father in heaven."

But God is a spirit, and a spirit can be both female and male. Sometimes the Bible says God's love and actions are like those of a woman and a mother.

So, girls (and boys), just remember that according to the Bible both Adam and Eve (female and male human beings) were made in the image of God. If both were originally like God, then God must be both male and female. Right?

What is the Holy Spirit?

The spirit of a person is the life of a person and what the person is like. The Spirit of God is what God is like in all His actions. God's Spirit, the Holy Spirit, is GOD.

Does the Holy Ghost look like Casper— white sheet and all?

Of course not. The Holy Ghost is the same as the Holy Spirit—the Spirit of God.

One of the Ten Commandments says, "You should have no other gods before me." What does that mean?

Whatever we value, whatever we think is important, whatever seems good to us can become a god to us. And when we think something or someone is more important than God, His love, and our life with Him, that something becomes a false god, an idol.

It might be money, fun, a house, a job, or even a pet. It could be a person—even you yourself. It could be anything.

Who or what do you love most? That's the question. And the answer will tell you what false gods you may be worshiping.

Is it true that God helps those who help themselves?

If you think the statement says that God helps those who are grabby and selfish, then it's not true. If you think it says that God usually helps the people who are willing to do their part, then it's true. Of course, God also helps people who cannot help themselves.

If God can do anything, why didn't He make my mother well?

We could ask, "Why doesn't God make everybody well?" He's working at it. He wants all people to be healthy, not sick. In heaven there is no sin or sickness. But until God changes this world into a heavenly place, there will be sickness of many kinds. In the meantime He wants us to do what we can to help people get well and stay well.

If God has the power to turn bad things into something good, why doesn't He?

He does. For instance, when a man lost his job, he got a better one; and when a church burned down, the people built a new one. Paul was a bad man God turned into a good person. He wrote in the Bible, "We know that in everything God works for good with those who love Him." (Romans 8:28)

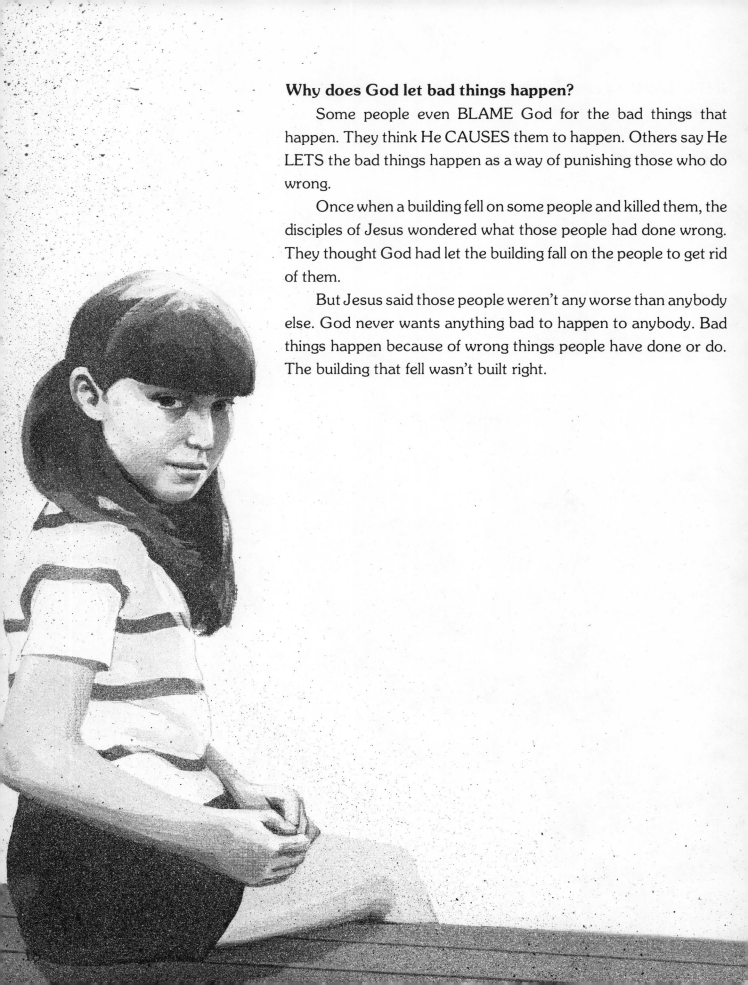

Why does God let bad things happen?

Some people even BLAME God for the bad things that happen. They think He CAUSES them to happen. Others say He LETS the bad things happen as a way of punishing those who do wrong.

Once when a building fell on some people and killed them, the disciples of Jesus wondered what those people had done wrong. They thought God had let the building fall on the people to get rid of them.

But Jesus said those people weren't any worse than anybody else. God never wants anything bad to happen to anybody. Bad things happen because of wrong things people have done or do. The building that fell wasn't built right.

Where was God when my friend was hit by a car?

God is everywhere at all times. A psalm in the Bible says that we can't go anywhere where God is not. You may want to read this for yourself. It's Psalm 139:7-10.

In another psalm God said:

>Because he (a person) loves Me
>I will rescue him.
>I will protect him because he knows Me.
>When he calls to Me, I will answer him.
>I will be with him in trouble.
>I will rescue him and honor him.
>
> Psalm 91:14-16 (HBFC)

Now read the psalm verses again. This time substitute "she" for "he" and "her" for "him." Then ask yourself, "Who helped your friend when she was hit by a car?" God was acting *through those people.*

My teacher said God lives in people.
Does God live in me?

God lives in *some* people—the people who believe in Jesus. If you believe that Jesus is God, then God lives in you. The Bible says, "No one can say 'Jesus is Lord' (and really mean it) unless he is directed by the Holy Spirit" (1 Corinthians 12:3). The Holy Spirit is God in the persons who believe that Jesus is God.

**People say that God loves everybody,
but does He love killers too?**

God doesn't like anything that is wrong. This includes anything wrong that we may do. People who kill other people make God very sad and sometimes very angry. God told the prophet Isaiah to write, "I, the Lord, love justice. I hate robbery and wrong" (Isaiah 61:8). But Jesus showed us how God also loves and forgives. He even asked God to forgive the people who killed Him.

If I do something very bad, will God punish me?

We've all done things that were wrong. Have you ever taken something that didn't belong to you? Have you ever cheated on a test? Lied to your parents? If you were caught, you were probably punished. But did God, who knows all things, forgive you? That's the important question.

We can be sure that God is merciful and kind. The Bible says, "God loved us and sent His Son to pay for our sins" (1 John 4:10 HBFC). For Jesus' sake He forgives whatever we do wrong when we are sorry about what we've done. And that's really good news. That's why it's called the Gospel.

**Why doesn't God get rid of all bad people
and let only the good people live?**

Once when some people wouldn't let Jesus come to their village, two of His disciples wanted God to punish them by sending fire down on them from the sky. But Jesus scolded them for wanting this. If God would punish all people whenever they did wrong, we would all be punished often. You wouldn't want that, would you? Be glad that God is forgiving and patient. He keeps on hoping we'll change for the better, as you'll see by reading Luke 13:6-9.

**If God loves and protects us,
why doesn't He warn us when an earthquake
is going to happen, or a flood, or a tornado?**

First of all we need to remember what the apostle Paul wrote in his letter to the Romans. "I am certain," he said, "that nothing can separate us from the love of Christ" (Romans 8:38). And God usually does warn people of dangers and coming disasters through some of the technology man has created. When a disaster does happen, God's love gets to work at once and helps His children in their trouble.

Does God ever get angry and punish people?

Oh yes. The Bible says that God is long-suffering, but His patience sometimes comes to an end. Sooner or later people who don't love God and break His laws have to suffer for what they do wrong. God told one of His prophets in the Old Testament to write this very clearly so that people would be sure to understand it. "This is the message," wrote the prophet. "Those who are evil will not survive" (Habakkuk 2:4). Even Christians who ask and receive God's forgiveness sometimes have to suffer on earth for what they do wrong.

I'm afraid of thunderstorms.
Is God angry when it storms?

You needn't be afraid of thunder. It's only a sound caused by a sudden expansion of air that follows a flash of lightning.

Once God sent a strong wind against a mountain when the prophet Elijah was hiding in a cave. But the Bible says that God was not in the wind. After the wind came an earthquake and then a fire. But God was not in the earthquake or fire. Then Elijah heard a small quiet voice. When Elijah heard the soft voice that told him not to be afraid, he knew it was God speaking to him.

God usually isn't in the bad things that happen. God is good. But you can always hear Him in what he says about His love for you.

The grace of God—what's that?

Many people say grace before eating. In this case grace is a short prayer of thanks for food. But the grace of God is something quite different.

Jesus once told a story about a man who owed his king more than he could ever pay. When the man begged for mercy, the king forgave the whole debt. He wiped it out. That was grace—the kind of grace God is willing to give to anyone who really wants it. Grace is not just love; it's love with mercy—forgiving love.

You can read the story in Luke 7:36-50. And remember that God is gracious.

Is God against people going to other planets?

Some people used to say, "If God had wanted us to fly, He would have given us wings." In a way God *did* give people wings by making it possible for them to fly in airplanes and spaceships. And God's plans for people were not all completed in the past. His greatest wonders are still to come. If God doesn't want us to live on the moon it won't happen. But maybe He does!

Can I be sure God will help me when I need help?

In Psalm 91 God says, "I will save those who love Me and will protect those who know Me as Lord. When they call to Me, I will answer them; when they are in trouble, I will be with them. I will rescue them and honor them. I will reward them with long life; I will save them." (Psalm 91:14-16)

24

**Why did God create mice and roaches and fleas
and things like that?**

Everything in God's world serves a good purpose, even if we
don't know what that purpose is. Mice, for example, are food for
some other animals and birds. They are used by scientists for
testing medicines before these are given to humans. Roaches warn
people that there may be spoiled food standing around, and they
too are food for birds and animals.

About Jesus

Was Jesus God?

When Jesus was born in Bethlehem, an angel appeared to some shepherds and said, "This very day, in King David's town, the Savior, Christ the Lord, was born" (Luke 2:11). One day, after Jesus had started teaching and healing people, He asked His friend Peter, "Who do you say I am?" Peter answered, "You are the Christ, the Son of the Living God." (Matthew 16:16)

In many ways the Bible says that Jesus was God's Son living on earth as a human being. But the Bible also says, "Think the way Jesus Christ thought. Even though He was like God, He didn't think that being equal with God was what was most important. No, He gave it all up and became a servant. . . . This is why God highly honored Jesus and gave Him a name that is greater than any other name." (Philippians 2:5)

Why is Jesus called the Savior?

In the Hebrew language the name Jesus means a person who saves. When an angel of God told Joseph that his wife Mary would have a son, the angel said, "Name Him Jesus, because He will save His people from their sins" (Matthew 1:21). Jesus said, "I came to save the world." (John 12:47)

What does it mean to believe in Jesus?

To believe in Jesus could mean simply agreeing with what He taught and did. But when the Bible and Christians talk about believing in Jesus, they especially mean being *sure* that Jesus is the Son of God and the person God sent to be the Savior of the world. Having faith in Jesus is also trusting (that is, counting on) His power and love and His promises of forgiveness and care.

Was Jesus really born on the 25th day of December?

Jesus was really born. The Christmas story in the Bible tells us where He was born and what happened when He was born. But the date on which He was born is not mentioned in the Bible, so no one can say exactly when it was.

In the year 354 A.D. a pope chose December 25 as the birthday of Jesus so that all Christians could celebrate it together. But some celebrate it on January 6. The exact date is not important. What is important is that we know and believe that Jesus came to be our Savior.

Was Jesus a normal kid?

That depends on what you mean by normal. Jesus was a real human being. The Bible tells us He was born in Bethlehem, lived in Egypt for a while, and later returned to a town in Palestine called Nazareth, where He learned to be a carpenter. Up to about age 30 we might say that Jesus lived a normal life, much like that of other Hebrew children in His day. Still, the Bible also says, "He was tempted in *every* way we are tempted, but He didn't sin (Hebrews 4:15 HBFC). And that, you know, isn't normal.

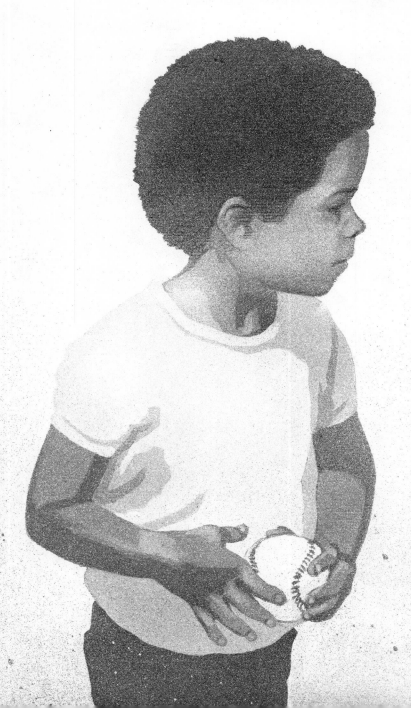

Did Jesus have any brothers and sisters?

He probably did, but we can't be sure. The Bible says that once when Jesus was talking to people, His mother and brothers arrived. But in Bible times brothers also meant other relatives. While they waited outside the place where Jesus was speaking, someone said to Him, "Your mother and brothers are standing outside; they want to talk to you." Jesus pointed to His disciples and said, "Whoever does what My Father in heaven wants him to do is My brother, My sister, and My mother." (Matthew 12:59 TEV)

Did Jesus have any children?

Jesus never married, so He didn't have any children as the father of a family. But He sometimes called His followers His children. For example, He said, "My children, I shall not be with you very much longer" (John 13:33). In that meaning Jesus had and still has many many children.

Did Jesus ever have any fun?

That depends on what is meant by fun. Jesus often talked about His joy and the joys of His followers. He must have been a happy person because people enjoyed being around Him. People don't enjoy being with an unhappy person.

Did Jesus say He was God?

Many times in the New Testament Jesus is *called* the Son of God. And Jesus himself said He was the Christ, the promised Savior and Son of God. He also said, "I and the Father are one," and many other such statements.

**What did Jesus mean when He said,
"Whoever has seen Me has seen the Father?"**

Jesus meant what He said. He meant that He and God the Father were alike. He, the Son of God, was God living on earth as a human being. He said that the Father was living in Him. Those who learn to know Jesus learn to know God. You can read about this in John 14:5-11.

Why is Jesus sometimes called Lord?

A lord is a ruler. People in the Old Testament called God their Lord. Christians who call Jesus their Lord are saying that He is their God and the ruler of their lives.

If Jesus is God, did He pray to Himself?

No, He prayed to His Father in heaven. You see, the God of Christians is a triune God—three persons: Father, Son, and Holy Spirit. Jesus is God the Son.

Why was Jesus crucified?

Several different answers could be given. First of all, the leaders of the city of Jerusalem wanted to get rid of Jesus. They were afraid He might take over the government. They were also afraid He was changing the people's religion. But the Bible gives the reason Jesus *allowed* Himself to be put to death on a cross. It says, "Christ died for everyone so that those who live would no longer live for themselves, but for Him who died for them." (1 Corinthians 5:15)

If Jesus had the power to save Himself, why didn't He?

As Jesus was hanging on a cross, people walking by said sneeringly, "Save Yourself if You are God's Son! Come on down from the cross!" And the priests and religion teachers made fun of Him saying, "He saved others, but He can't save Himself!" (Matthew 27:40-42). The Gospel truth is that if Jesus had saved Himself He would not have saved us. The Bible says, "Jesus died for us in order that we might live together with Him." (1 Thessalonians 5:10 TEV)

What were the last words Jesus said on the cross?

When you read an announcement about the "seven last words of Jesus," it doesn't mean single words. It refers to seven different statements Jesus made before He died. The very last words were, "Father, into Your hands I put My spirit" (Luke 23:46 HBFC). After saying this, He died.

Why did Jesus wash the feet of His disciples?

Jesus explained why He had washed His disciples' feet during the last supper He had with them. He said to them, "I have given you an example" (John 13:15). It was an example of serving others. Jesus wanted His disciples to learn to serve others.

Will Jesus come again? Some say He's here now.

Before disappearing into heaven Jesus told His disciples, "Remember this: I am with you always, and I will be to the end of time" (Matthew 28:20 HBFC). Jesus is living here on earth right now in many ways, but His resurrected body is not in any one place.

What is "the world to come"?
I thought there was only one world.

Actually there are many kinds of worlds. We can talk about the animal kingdom, the plant world, the world of the stars, etc. The world to come could be future life on earth or it could mean a person's life after death. When Christians talk about the world without end, they mean the life that God rules with His Spirit, the kingdom of heaven in which Jesus is the king.

What happened to all the people who lived
before Jesus came and died for them?

We know Abraham and Moses and Elijah and many others who lived before Jesus lived on earth are in heaven. The New Testament mentions them as being with God. Their sins were forgiven by the same God who forgives us our sins for Jesus' sake. They believed that God would someday send a Savior.

About Sin and Forgiveness

What is sin?

Sin, the Bible says, is the breaking of God's laws. Since His laws are all summed up in that one word "love," sin is any kind of failure to love God and people. Sin is hating and harming people. Sin is everything evil—the opposite of what is good.

Is there such a thing as a little sin?

All sins are wrong—and they are crimes against God. So in one way of thinking, there are no little sins. All sins are serious because they may separate us from life with God.

But there is of course a difference between burning someone's house down and just making a nasty remark. Both are sins. But some sins do more harm than others. Happily for us all, God is willing to forgive our big sins as well as our little sins.

Is it a sin to swear if I don't take God's name in vain?

People who swear on a Bible or with their hand raised ask God to be the judge of what they are saying. They may even ask God to punish them if what they are saying or promising isn't true. If they don't mean it, they are taking God's name in vain.

Some swearing is cursing. Cursing is wishing something bad for someone else—like "God damn you" or "To hell with you." Almost all cursing is a sin, whether it uses God's name or not, because it's usually a hate-wish instead of a love-wish. Only loving thoughts, words, and deeds please God.

In Matthew 5:34-37 Jesus advised us not to swear at all when making a promise. "Just say 'Yes' or 'No'—he said. Anything else you say comes from the Evil One."

My friend says it's against the law to eat pork.
We ate pork chops last night.
Did we do something wrong?

No law in our country forbids eating pork. But some religions have a law against it. The friend is probably a Jew whose parents try to keep the laws of the Old Testament. Or the friend may be a Muslim whose parents obey the laws of their holy book called the Koran.

In the Old Testament God told His people not to eat pork, but Jesus and the New Testament freed people from such laws. You can see for yourself by reading Colossians 2:15.

My parents are divorced. Are they sinners?

All people are sinners. In other words, we all do wrong things and need forgiveness. The Bible says that usually God wants married people to stay together. They promised God they would when they got married. But sometimes a divorce occurs. When it does, God loves the divorced people the same as He loves married and single people. That's good to know.

Are people who work on Sundays committing a sin?

Lots of Christians used to believe that it's wrong to work on Sundays. Some still do. People called Seventh Day Adventists and very religious Jews think that working on Saturday is a breaking of God's law.

In the Old Testament there is a law that says, "Remember the Sabbath Day, to keep it holy." And there were laws against doing almost anything on the Sabbath Day, the day for rest. But Jesus freed us from such laws and taught us to do good things for people on any day. You can check this by reading Matthew 12:1-13.

**When I say "Gosh" and "Gee" and "Golly,"
are those bad words? My grandma says they are.**

The word "gosh" is probably a substitute for God and "gee" is a shortened form of the name Jesus. Most people who say those words don't know what they are saying. They are just surprise words, or words that let out some steam.

Your grandmother doesn't want you to use names for God without a good reason. One of God's commandments says, "Do not take the name of the Lord, your God, in vain. In vain means for no good reason.

Why do people steal and kill?

The next time you see someone doing something wrong, ask him or her why they are doing it. Why do children throw stones at windows or break signs or write on buildings or take things in stores? Why do some children enjoy hurting others by pushing or hitting or telling lies? You'll probably get a lot of different answers. Some will say they don't know why. Others will give you a poor excuse. No matter what they say, they're just not loving God and caring about other people.

Is it all right to get angry?

That depends on whether we have a good reason for getting angry. We ought to get angry over things that aren't right. Jesus did. But the Bible tells us not to get angry too easily—not to *lose* our temper (James 1:19). And it also says in Ephesians 4:26, "If you become angry, do not let your anger lead you into sin," especially the sin of hurting and not forgiving people.

Why doesn't God make people be good instead of letting them do bad things?

God doesn't force people to be good. People who are good only when they have to be really aren't good. But when they learn how good and loving God is and start to love God, they begin to get His Spirit. God's Spirit, the Holy Spirit, makes people at least a little like God. That's the way God makes them good.

In Bible days some men had lots of wives.
If it's wrong *now*, why wasn't it wrong *then*?

In Bible times having more than one wife wasn't against the law of the country the way it is now in our country. There are still some places, especially in Africa, where men may have several wives. But God gave Adam only one wife, so that's probably what God planned as best for people in all times and places.

What does covet mean?

To covet means to desire something very much. Not all wanting is wrong, but several of God's commandments forbid coveting what belongs to someone else. Wanting becomes wrong especially when it includes trying to get what we want away from the person who has it and doesn't want to part with it.

What makes people jealous?

A jealous person doesn't like anyone else to have something he or she doesn't have. That something could be anything—an ability, a friend, money, or clothes. Jealous persons want to be first and want the most. It's really their selfishness that makes them jealous.

What's the difference between a soldier killing people in war and just plain murder?

Not all killing is murder. When a policeman shoots a robber who is running away, that's not the same as a robber shooting a policeman or a person being robbed. In the kingdom of God there is no killing. But when a government orders its soldiers to fight for their country, they sometimes have to kill.

I love to talk. Is talking too much a sin?

Too much of anything isn't good, but talking usually can be a very good thing. It can be a way of loving other people. A person who refuses to talk to another person or just doesn't isn't as friendly as the one who does.

Is there any sure way to keep from sinning?

No matter what people do, they can't keep from sinning. Because no human being is perfect, no one can do anything perfectly.

But there is a sure way to have forgiveness for all sins. Jesus said, "I am the Way." He gives people God's forgiveness when they believe His promises.

Jesus also gives the Holy Spirit to those who love Him, and that keeps them from sinning.

My father sins. Will he go to heaven?

Everybody sins. If people who sin can't go to heaven, no one will. Jesus gives life with God to all who believe in Him, and that life with God is heaven.

About Being a Christian

Am I a Christian?

A person isn't a Christian just by being a good person or by belonging to a church. Some persons who aren't Christians may be nicer or kinder than those who are. And not everyone who believes in God or belongs to a church is a Christian.

Jesus once said, "My sheep listen to My voice . . . and they follow Me" (John 10:27 TEV). Christians are the people who believe that Jesus is the Son of God and Savior of the world. They also follow (that means, they try to do) His teachings because they love Him. So now it's up to you to decide whether you are a Christian.

What can *I* do for God?

The question sounds as though there isn't much that most persons can do for God. But anyone can do for God whatever he or she does. That means, we can love God by whatever we do and by the way we do what we do.

How can I know what God wants me to do?

You won't be able to know everything God wants you to do, but you *usually* can know what His will is. In both the Old and New Testament there is a Golden Rule. It can be said in many ways. Jesus said it this way: "Do for others what you want them to do for you" (Matthew 7:12 TEV). In other words, "Treat other people the way you would like to be treated by them." In the Old Testament the Law was, "Love your neighbor as you love yourself" (Matthew 22:39 TEV). When you follow this rule you'll be doing what God wants you to do.

When the Bible tells me to love my neighbor, what does that mean?

Jesus said there are two great commandments of God that include all the others. The first one tells you to love God more than anything or anyone else. The second says, "Love your neighbor as (the way you love) yourself."

Your neighbors aren't just the people who live next door to you. It's ALL the people who live around you and also in other neighborhoods. In fact, it's the people anywhere and everywhere. To love them is to do only what will do them some good.

I know the Bible tells us to love everybody.
But can I be a Christian and not LIKE everybody?

People don't become Christians by what they do. It's faith in Jesus that makes you a Christian and not whether you love or like everybody. Jesus helps you to LOVE other people, but He doesn't even *want* you to *like* what some of them do. Of course, if "like" means being friendly, that's a different matter.

How can I love someone who hates me?

Our Lord Jesus said, "If you love only people who love you, why should anyone praise or reward you for that? Even rascals do that! And if you greet only your friends, what more are you doing than others do? . . . You are to be perfect, just as your Father in heaven is perfect" (Matthew 5:46-48 HBFC). That's why Jesus said, "Love your enemies and pray for those who hate and hurt you. In that way you will be the sons (and daughters) of your Father in heaven" (Matthew 5:44, 45 HBFC). How can we do that? By asking God to help us.

What's a talent and who has it?

A talent is a special ability that God gives to people. For this reason talents are also called gifts. A gifted person has many talents. Everybody has at least one talent—a special ability to do something. Most people have several talents. God wants us to use whatever talents he gives us.

How can I know what's right and fair?

Everybody has some idea of what's right and fair. Most people, even if they aren't Christians, know that it's wrong to hurt another person.

It's never wrong to love the way God loves. And Jesus said that God's Spirit will show you what is right. So, to know what is right, you need to receive the spirit of God.

Why is it better to give than to receive?

Jesus didn't say it was better. He said it's more blessed. That means, "Giving makes you more happy than receiving." Why? It just does. Maybe it's because giving is a kind of loving.

Do I have to go to church to be a Christian?

There are some Christians who never go to church. They are Christians because they believe that Jesus is their Savior, and they have faith in His promises and teachings. They don't go to church because they can't.

Going to church doesn't decide whether you are a Christian. But going to church and learning God's Word can *help* you be a Christian. And people who really love God feel the way the psalm writer did who wrote, "I was glad when they said to me, 'Let us go to the Lord's house.' " (Psalm 122:1 TEV)

What will make me happy?

If you're selfish, nothing will make you happy. But God can make you happy. The Bible says, "Trust in the Lord and you will be happy" (Proverbs 16:20). Also doing what God wants you to do will make you happy, especially doing things for other people. Try it; you'll see.

How do people become saints?

A lot of children think that saints are people who are goody-good. Some persons are called saints after they die because of good things they did while they were living. But the Bible calls all Christians "saints" because God forgives their sins for Jesus' sake. With all their sins forgiven, people are holy in God's sight. That's like a loving mother who thinks her child is perfect. She forgives and overlooks what is wrong.

Is it true that when I *think* bad things, it's as bad as *doing* bad things?

That depends. Both are wrong. But if a person *does* something wrong without knowing it or wanting to, that's not as bad as *planning* to do the wrong and *wanting* to do it. The Bible says that wrong actions are caused by wrong thoughts and feelings. (Mark 7:21)

I stole a comic book in a drug store once. No one saw me and I'm sorry I did it. But it still bothers me. Why?

As you can see, whenever anyone does something wrong, just being sorry doesn't straighten things out. First of all, we need forgiveness. And thank God, He's always willing to forgive those who are sorry and want forgiveness. Believing that good news gives a person peace.

But there's also something else that will help straighten out what you've done wrong. You can try to make amends; that means, mend or repair what you've done wrong. In the case of the stolen comic book, you could go and pay for it, as you should have in the first place. You'll feel better after you've paid for what you've stolen.

Is cleanliness really next to godliness?

A lot of people used to think that the saying "Cleanliness is next to godliness" is in the Bible, but it's not. John Wesley, a Methodist minister in England, once made the statement in a sermon, and other people began to repeat it.

Is it true? Is keeping your body and your clothes clean almost as important as being godly? Of course not. Often the persons willing to let themselves get dirty are more helpful to others than those who want to stay clean and pretty.

It's all right to be clean, but just being clean and dressed up doesn't make a person good or godly.

Why did God make me the way I am?

God may not be the one who made you the way you are. It's true that God has given human beings the kind of body they have. The psalm writer said in Psalm 139 that we have all been wonderfully made by God. And it's also true that God played a

part in making us what we are even before we were born. But don't blame God for anything you think is wrong. He may not want you to be the way you are. And he'll gladly change you for the better if you want him to do so.

What's an atheist?

An atheist (AYE-thee-ist) is a person who believes that there is no God. People who call themselves atheists at least *say* they don't believe there is a God.

**I read a book about Christian presidents
and Thomas Jefferson wasn't included.
They said he was a deist. What's that?**

A deist (DEE-ist) believes there is a God, a deity, but a deist thinks of God mainly as a good and powerful spirit. He doesn't think Jesus is God, nor does he think the Bible is the Word of God.

How can I be sure I'm not believing a false prophet?

Jesus said we could recognize false prophets by their fruits; that means by looking at what their teachings produce. He said a good tree produces good fruit, but weeds and thistles only produce more weeds. The same is true of good teachers and false prophets.

What does it mean to keep the faith?

When people say, "Keep the faith, Baby," they aren't talking about any certain kind of faith. They just mean, "Keep on hoping everything will turn out all right, maybe even the way you want it to be." They may also mean, "Keep on truckin' "; that is, keep on living as though everything will be all right. But to have faith in Jesus means more than just hoping something will happen. Faith in Jesus is believing that He is our Savior and Lord.

My teacher told me to let my conscience be my guide. What's my conscience?

Conscience is that certain something in a person that tells what is right and wrong. Some people have a poorly developed conscience, a weak conscience. But everybody has some ideas of right and wrong. Even though these ideas aren't always true, it's better to follow your conscience and do what you think is right rather than do what you think is wrong.

Is it all right to fail?

Everybody fails to be perfect, and most of us fail many times before we learn to do something well. Babies fall down often and have to keep trying in order to learn how to walk. Tennis players or any other kind of athlete have to keep trying in order to get good. And no athlete wins all the time. God forgives our failures and helps us when we ask Him to do so.

**If my parents are Christians,
how come they often get angry at me?**

That's hard to tell. Sometimes parents get so busy or so worried, they forget how to love. Or they love their children so much that they want them to be perfect. And sometimes children forget to love their parents. That too spells trouble for the children as well as their parents.

**Why should we share what God gives us?
Doesn't He want us to have what He gives?**

Sure He wants us to have what He gives, but He gives us His gifts for good purposes. And one of His good purposes is to benefit others as well as ourselves through what He gives us. The Bible says, "God loves the one who gives gladly. And God is able to give you more than you need for yourselves and more than enough for every good cause." (2 Corinthians 9:7, 8)

What does it mean to tithe?

Tithing is giving a tenth of one's income to the work of the church and other good purposes. A tenth of a dollar would be 10 cents; a tenth of ten dollars would be a dollar.

In the Old Testament, tithing was a law. The children of Israel paid their priests and took care of the temple by giving a tenth of what they earned.

Some churches still make tithing a law, but Jesus freed His followers from such laws. He wants Christians to be ruled by the love of God. That's why some Christians gladly give more than a tithe when they can. In Mark 12:41-44 you can read a story about a widow who gave God a lot more than a tithe.

About Churches and Worship

What does the word "denomination" mean?

A denomination is an organization that unites a number of congregations (local churches) into a body with a general name, like the American Lutheran Church, the Roman Catholic Church, the Southern Baptists, the United Church of Christ. Some denominations are related; for example, all Lutherans or all Baptists or all Mennonites. Their members have some common beliefs and some common ways of worshiping.

Why are there so many different kinds of churches?

There are many different groups (or denominations) within the church of Jesus Christ—some small, some very large. And there are many different reasons for these separate groups.

But understood in a certain way, there is only one Christian church—one large body of people who are believers and followers of Jesus. The Bible says, "There is one Lord, one faith, one baptism, one God and Father of all." (Ephesians 5:5 HBFC)

Will something bad happen to me if I miss church?

First of all, God couldn't care less about your going to church if you don't love Him and don't want to worship Him. Furthermore, God is a loving, forgiving God, so He also forgives your missing church. But that doesn't mean He doesn't miss you and that you don't miss something important when you miss church.

Is it all right to have friends who don't go to church?

Jesus was a friend to a lot of people who didn't go to a church. He was called a friend of sinners. And anyway, just going to church may not make you any better than those who don't. But by being a good friend to others who don't go to church, you may be able to get them to go with you. That way they'll learn to know your Lord Jesus and may become Christians.

Do I have to dress up to go to church?

Years ago most people wore their best clothes to church on Sundays. That's why they called those clothes their "Sunday best." But a lot of people today don't like to dress up. It makes them feel stiff and uncomfortable. And what we wear probably doesn't matter at all to God as long as it is not indecent. In the Bible God said to the prophet Samuel, "Man looks at the outward appearances, but I look at the heart" (1 Samuel 16:7). It's your heart that God cares about.

Why do some people go to church on Saturdays and some on Sundays?

In the Old Testament one of the ten commandments God gave to his people was, "Remember the Sabbath Day, to keep it holy." The Sabbath Day was Saturday, the seventh day of the week. Religious Jews still obey that commandment. So do people who call themselves Seventh Day Adventists. But Christians made Sunday, the first day of the week, a special day for coming together to worship God. Sundays remind them that Jesus came out of His grave alive on that day.

Is it wrong to laugh in church?

God wants people to be happy. Jesus said He came to make people happy. Christians ought to be the happiest people in the world, because they know how much God loves them.

Happy people often laugh. People who are afraid to laugh or hardly ever laugh aren't happy.

The Bible says, "Be happy with Jesus." So it must be all right to laugh in church unless the laughing disturbs others or makes fun of someone else.

Why don't some people sing in the church service?

Good question. Perhaps some people don't sing because they have a sore throat or a cold. Older people may not be able to see and read the words. Some people don't like to try to sing a hymn they don't know. But why a lot of others don't sing is a mystery. And it's a pity, because they're probably not worshiping God as happily as they would if they sang along with those whose do.

What is a seminary?

A seminary is a school where people who want to become pastors study for several years after finishing college. Usually seminary students must also serve a congregation as a vicar or intern for one year before becoming a pastor. During that time they get training and supervision under a pastor. After students graduate from a seminary they are either placed in a position or they are chosen by a congregation.

Who is a "man of the cloth"?

The words "man of the cloth" are another name for a minister, a clergyman. People probably began to use this title for a pastor or priest because of the "cloth" they wore and still wear. This cloth is, of course, the robe or robes.

What does a minister do all week?

Not all ministers do the same thing, and no minister does the same work every day. Some spend time studying and preparing their church services. Many pastors visit their church members who are in the hospital and call on people who have visited their services. Sometimes they conduct wedding and funeral services and prepare for meetings they must lead or attend. They also try to

help people who are having trouble and they teach a confirmation or membership class. Many serve on community projects to help improve the lives of people. Most pastors are very busy during the week as well as on Sundays, but they are happy in serving God and his people.

Are only pastors and priests allowed to preach in a church?

Every Christian is to be a minister; that is, a servant of God and other people. But ordinarily only those who are trained by the church and are chosen by a congregation have the right to lead the services and preach in a church. Other members may lead parts of the service and may speak to the congregation on special occasions if they are asked or when a trained pastor is not available.

Why do churches baptize people?

Probably the first reason why Christians baptize people is that Jesus told His followers to do just that. He said, "The right to rule everything in heaven and on earth has been given to Me. Therefore go to people everywhere in the world and make them My disciples. Baptize them in the name of the Father and of the Son and of the Holy Spirit." (Matthew 28:19 HBFC)

Baptism makes people disciples of Jesus and members of His church. But that's not all it does. It also gives people God's forgiveness of sins. That's like God washing away everything wrong in a person's life. What could be better than that?

Can children be baptized without their parent's permission?

When children are no longer under the care of their parents, they certainly can be baptized without their parents' permission. But as long as parents are in charge of their children, no one has a right to baptize them without the parents' permission. Furthermore, children who are baptized into the church of Jesus Christ are to be taught the Christian faith and life. For that the help of their parents is very important.

In some churches you can't take Communion until you're confirmed. Why is that?

There is no law in the Bible that says children must be confirmed before they can participate in Holy Communion. But St. Paul told the Corinthian Christians they should first examine themselves before eating the bread and drinking the wine. He warned them against eating and drinking the Lord's Supper without understanding its meaning. To help children understand what happens in Holy Communion, some churches require at least a short period of special instruction before allowing children to take Communion.

What is confirmation?

In Greek, Roman Catholic, and Anglican churches confirmation is thought to be a sacrament that gives children the gift of the Holy Spirit. The children are confirmed by a bishop laying his hand on them and blessing them. In the Lutheran church confirmation is a ceremony in which persons make a public confession of their faith before becoming adult members of a congregation. Not all churches have confirmation because there is no law in the Bible that says it has to be done.

What is the Apostles' Creed?

It is a statement of what Christians believe about God and His great acts of creation, the saving of the world, and the blessings of the Holy Spirit. It is called the *Apostles'* Creed because it is based on the teachings of the apostles of Jesus in the Bible.

What's the communion of saints?

Communion means "in union with." All Christians are united with each other in one church by being baptized into the same family of God and by having the same Lord. Those who are saints all have the same faith in God's forgiveness of their sins.

Christians are called saints because all their sins are forgiven. The church of which they all are members is called holy because God makes the members saints and gives them the Holy Spirit.

Did you know that you are a saint and a member of the holy church of Jesus Christ? Well, you are if you've been baptized and believe in Jesus and His Gospel of love and forgiveness.

What does the word "evangelical" mean?

The word "evangel" means "Gospel" in Greek. So an evangelical church is a church that is loyal to the Gospel of Jesus Christ and is directed by it. Some Christians who emphasize evangelism (that is, sharing the Gospel with others) call themselves evangelicals. All people who are really Christians could be called evangelicals.

Why do Roman Catholics call their church service a "mass"?

The word "mass" comes from the Latin word *missa*, which means "to send." Some scholars think that the word began to be used for a church service when the people who were not confirmed members were sent out before Holy Communion was celebrated by the congregation. This is no longer done, but the word is still used by Roman Catholics as a name for their services.

Is it okay for me to go to church if I have no money to put in the offering?

No one *has* to give an offering in church at any time. In fact, in the Bible God says he doesn't *even want* our offering if we don't love Him. The giving of an offering in a church service is like giving someone a present. As you know, presents are so much nicer when they're given with love.

Is it true that the more I give to the church, the more I'll get from God?

Probably not, if getting more for yourself is the reason you give to the church. But the apostle Paul did say in one of his letters, "Remember that the person who plants few seeds will have a small crop; the one who plants many seeds will have a large crop. Each one should give, then, as he has decided, not with regret or out of a sense of duty; for God loves the one who gives gladly. And God is able to give you more than you need, so that you will always have all you need for yourselves and more than enough for every good cause." (2 Corinthians 9:6-8 TEV)

Why is Easter on a different day every year?

When Christians began celebrating the resurrection of their Lord Jesus from the dead on a certain day of the year, some chose the 14th day of the fourth month. This put Easter on a different day of the week each year.

But most Christians wanted Easter on a Sunday, the first day of the week. So in the year 325 the ruler Constantine arranged a meeting of church leaders to settle the matter. The meeting was called the Council of Nicaea (Nigh-SEE-ah). The council decided that Easter was to be on a Sunday and on the same Sunday all over the world.

The day chosen was the first Sunday after the first full moon in the spring. (It's called the vernal equinox.) But the first full moon in the spring is not on the same calendar date of every year. That's why the date of Easter changes a little from year to year between March 22 and April 25.

What is Lent?

Lent is the 40 weekdays before Easter. It's a special time for remembering the suffering and death of Jesus and that He gave His life to save people from their sins.

Why is the first day of Lent called Ash Wednesday?

In the beginning years of the church some Christians sprinkled ashes on their heads to show their feelings about their sins. This had been done also in Old Testament times. When that custom died out the Roman Catholic church started to put a mark with ashes on the foreheads of the people who came to Holy Communion on the first day of Lent. That's why that day is called Ash Wednesday. The mark is a reminder of the sins that caused the suffering and death of Jesus. This custom is still carried out in Roman Catholic and Anglican churches and also in some Lutheran churches.

About the Bible and Prayer

What's the Bible?

The Bible is a collection of books (writings). Some of them are ancient history; some are poetry and wise sayings; some tell the life of Jesus (biography); and some are epistles (letters). Still others are writings of prophets.

Why is the Bible called God's book?

Even though all the books of the Bible were written by human beings, Christians believe that God directed the authors to write what He wanted them to write. The Bible says, "Above everything else you must understand this: that no teaching of Scripture is simply a matter of someone's own opinion. No prophet's message ever came just by someone wanting to write. But men spoke a message that came from God when the Holy Spirit directed them" (2 Peter 1:21 HBFC). Because the Holy Spirit directed the writers to write the thoughts and the words that they wrote, their books are actually messages from God. That's why they are called God's Word and God's book.

Who put the 66 Bible books together?

No one knows for sure. Bible scholars believe that the Old Testament collection was made about 400 years before Jesus lived on earth. The writings called the New Testament were all written during the first 100 years after Jesus' birth. But it took several hundred more years before Christians took for granted that all 27 books were inspired by God.

Why is the Bible divided into two parts?

The 66 books of the Bible are grouped together in two sections. The first 39 books were written at different times before Jesus was born. They are called the Old Testament. The last 27 books or letters were written after Jesus was born. Together they are called the New Testament.

What's a testament?

It's not a test. The word means an agreement, a statement with a promise. Another big word with somewhat the same meaning is covenant (KUV-eh-nant).

The Old Testament books tell of agreements God made with the people of Israel. He promised He would be their God if they would obey Him and be true to Him. The New Testament tells of another kind of promise God made—the promise to be the God for all the people of the world who would believe and follow His Son Jesus.

God talked to Moses and Abraham and to other people in the Bible. Does He talk to people today?

God speaks to all of His people. Sometimes He speaks through happenings, as He did to Moses. Sometimes His voice is heard in our minds and in our hearts—our thoughts and feelings. And always He speaks through His words in the Bible and through the preaching and teaching of the Bible. But of course we have to understand the words of the Bible in order to really hear what God says in the Bible. That's why we need to study the Bible prayerfully.

What's the Gospel?

Gospel means "good news." Originally the word was godspel—*god* meaning "good" and *spel,* like in spelling, meaning "words." The Gospel of Jesus Christ is the good news that God sent Jesus to save people from their sins and that God forgives all sins for Jesus' sake.

What's an epistle?

No, it isn't a gun. It's a message sent as a letter. The epistles read in churches are letters that are in the New Testament part of the Bible. Most of these were messages sent to Christians by the missionary who called himself Paul.

What is a prophet?

A prophet (pronounced PROF-it) is a teacher, but a special kind of teacher. In the Bible a true prophet was someone chosen by God to tell the people God's plans and desires. Prophets received their messages from God.

Jesus was the greatest prophet of all. There were also *false* prophets and there still are. They are people who claim to be talking for God even though they are not saying what is true.

What is a proverb?

The dictionary says that a proverb is a short, popular saying that expresses a truth. The book in the Bible called Proverbs is a collection of sayings that praise wisdom and give advice on many subjects. Read some of the Proverbs. You'll see how wise they are.

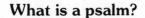

What is a psalm?

The Book of Psalms in the Bible is a collection of religious poems that the people of Israel used in their worship of God. Many of the psalms were written by King David. The psalms are still read, chanted, or sung in Christian services as well as by Jews in their religious services.

Why is the Bible sometimes called the King James Version?

Originally the books of the Old Testament were written in the Hebrew language. The New Testament books were written in Greek. Since the time when they were first written and collected, these books have been translated into many other languages.

In the year 1604 King James of England asked that an English translation of the whole Bible be made for use in the churches in England. This version is called the King James Version of the Bible. Today there are many other English translations or versions.

Which is the best version to use?

All versions of the Bible are translations of the same book. But some are more carefully done than others, and some are more readable than others. It's hard to say which version is best, but there are several that were written especially for children. They help children understand the Bible.

Is it wrong to burn a Bible?

If someone burns a Bible to show others his or her own feelings about the book, such action is disrespectful and very wrong. But if the Bible is worn out and is replaced with a newer copy, burning the old book is no worse than getting rid of it in some other way.

The Bible says I should be happy all the time.
How is that possible?

The Bible doesn't say we should be happy all the time. It says there is a time for laughing and a time for crying. We all ought to be sad about some things. But the Bible does say, "Be happy always in your life with the Lord" (Philippians 4:4 HBFC). People who live with the Lord can always be happy that they know Him.

Why should I pray?

There are many kinds of prayer and many reasons for praying. Prayer is talking to God. Sometimes prayer is asking God for help. Often we ought to be thanking God in prayer for blessings He gives without our asking Him. Always we have plenty of reasons just to think about God and to tell Him that we love Him. That's prayer, too, even though some people call it meditation.

What good does it do to pray?

That depends on how you pray. People who just mumble words and don't talk to God aren't really praying. And people who don't really mean what they pray can't expect any benefit from such prayers.

But the Bible says, "The prayer of a good person has a powerful effect" (James 5:16 TEV). Why? Because prayer puts such a person in touch with God. And God is powerful as well as good. He can and does answer the prayers of the people who believe in Him.

Do I have to kneel to pray?

No, and you don't have to stand either. Some people like to walk while they pray. Others pray while lying in bed on their backs. Some pray while they sit. You can suit yourself; God doesn't mind. God is interested in what you think and feel while you pray, not in the position of your body.

Is it necessary to pray every day?

Prayers are communications with God. If you love someone, you want to keep in touch with that person on a regular basis. So it is necessary to pray every day in order to keep in touch with God. But of course you don't *have* to, because it's not a law. God would rather hear you pray when you really *want* to.

Why do people say "Amen" at the end of prayers? Do I have to?

"Amen" is a Hebrew word. It means "Yes" and "May it be so." It's a short way of saying, "I agree" or "I really mean it." The word "amen" is used in the Bible in several places. But nowhere does it say you must use the word if you don't want to. In fact, now that you know what the word means, maybe there'll be times when you ought not say it.

What should I pray for?

Christians pray for anything they need or want. But they say what Jesus said when He prayed, "Not My will, but Yours be done."

Why doesn't God answer all prayers?

Jesus promised that God would answer all prayers prayed in His name; that means, by people who believe in Him. God listens to such prayers "for Jesus' sake." But always His answers are whatever is best in the long run. God doesn't simply do whatever we ask just because we think we are good Christians. God's goodness and love decide what He does and when. That's why we can be sure that when we pray, everything will turn out to be a blessing sooner or later.

The Lord's Prayer is said in different ways.
Which way is right?

Hardly anybody says the Lord's Prayer the way Jesus said it because he said it in Greek. Furthermore it appears in two different wordings in the Bible. You can see for yourself by looking at Matthew 6:9-13 and Luke 11:1-4. In addition, there are different translations of the Bible. So there is no single right way to say the Lord's Prayer. It can be said in many ways.

Jesus gave us His prayer as an example of what to pray for. So what's most important is that we pray for what He prayed. To do that we can use either His words or our own.

**At the end of the Lord's Prayer people say,
"For Thine is the kingdom and the power
and the glory." What is the kingdom?**

A kingdom is a country and people ruled by a king or queen. The kingdom for which Christians pray and which they say belongs to God is not a country. But it is people who let God rule them. In that kingdom or life God rules with His Spirit of love, which is powerful and wonderful. That's His glory.

About Angels and Devils and Heaven and Hell

What's an angel?

Sometimes children, especially babies, are called little angels, but they're not always angels. Angels often are pictured as people with wings, and that's not true either. The Bible says that angels are spirits sent by God to guard or help people or to bring people messages from God. They are forces that serve God.

Do angels have wings?

Angels don't have bodies of their own. They are spirits that live in other kinds of bodies. Artists sometimes picture angels as people with wings to show that they can move fast from one place to another, but they really don't have wings. Sometimes angels appear as human beings and are pictured as people, but they can also appear and serve God in other ways.

Are all angels white?

Since angels are spirits that can live in any kind of body, they don't have any certain color skin. White people usually picture angels as white, but they could just as well be pictured yellow, black, brown, or red.

Are angels male or female?

Spirits, good or bad, can be either male or female or both. They can live in either boys or girls, women or men. Most of the good angels mentioned in the Bible appeared in male bodies, but so did the bad ones. In pictures most of the good angels are women and girls, while the bad ones are men and boys. But it could also be the opposite.

Are there really angels all around us?

Jesus said there are many angels everywhere and that He could ask them to help Him anytime. The Bible says that God puts angels in charge of His children, to keep them from getting hurt or from hurting themselves.

Is there really such a thing as a guardian angel?

Psalm 91 says: "Because you made the Lord your shelter, the most high God your dwelling place, no harm will come to you, no great trouble will come near you. For God will put His angels in charge of you, to guard you wherever you go. They will hold you up with their hands so you won't stub your foot on a stone." (HBFC)

The devil quoted this passage to Jesus in tempting Him to jump from the highest part of the temple in Jerusalem. Some children like to think that because God's angels guard them, they can do anything they please and won't get hurt. That's foolish. Jesus told the devil, "The Scriptures also say, 'You must not test the Lord your God.' " (Luke 4:10 HBFC)

What are cherubs?

Sometimes a lovely child is called a cherub, or people say that a pretty child has the face of a cherub. But the word cherub means one of the cherubim, a group of angels mentioned in the Old Testament. They are not children or babies. They are spirits.

Is there really a devil?

You'd better believe it! According to the Bible there not only is a main devil, the chief of devils, called Satan; there are also many other devils or demons. They are wicked angels or spirits whose powers harm people. Many of these devils live in people and do their harm through people.

In Matthew 17:18 you can see that Jesus is more powerful than these spirits. When He spoke to the devils in people and ordered them out, they had to leave.

Does the devil look like
the pictures I've seen of him?

No matter what kind of pictures you've seen, they are just someone's way of showing the devil. You could make your own picture of him (or maybe he's a she sometimes).

Satan, another name for the devil, can be pictured in many different ways because the devil is a spirit. He is the chief of all evil spirits. A spirit doesn't have a body of its own. But it can get into the bodies of human beings and also into animals.

What do people mean when they say,
"The devil made me do it"?

People who say, "The devil made me do it," may just be giving an excuse for what they've done. They don't want to take the blame. But those who mean what they say believe that there is a devil who got them to do something they didn't really want to do.

**If God is more powerful than the devil,
why does He let him exist?**

This is a hard question to answer. God has put the devil out of
His kingdom called heaven. And He sent Jesus to drive the devil
out of people. When people let Jesus rule them, Jesus saves them
from the devil by destroying his power over them.

Are there really people who worship the devil?

Yes. There are people who even have a place where they pray to the devil and dance and play music to him. Maybe they think the devil won't hurt them if they honor and praise him (or her). Or maybe they really love an evil spirit and find it exciting. Too bad. The devil causes suffering and death.

Is it possible to sell your soul to the devil?

There are stories and plays in which people made a deal with the devil. They promised to let the devil rule them if he would give them certain favors they wanted. That's what is called selling your soul to the devil. It could happen in real life, and it does when people are willing to do wrong in order to get what they want.

My mother is going to have a baby. She said that the baby will be a gift from heaven. What does that mean?

A gift from heaven means a gift from God. God is the giver of life because all life comes from Him. So when a new baby is born, it's a wonderful gift from God, a gift from heaven.

Where is heaven?

Sometimes looking up to heaven (or the heavens) simply means looking at the sky. The kingdom of heaven that Jesus talked about is not a place above the clouds, like some people think. It's where God is and wherever Jesus rules.

What's heaven like?

The Bible describes heaven as a city with streets made of gold and walls built with jewels. You can read this picture of heaven in Revelation 21:18-21. The Bible also says that in that place there will be no more sickness or sadness or trouble and no more crying (Revelation 7:16, 17). Everything will be perfect and everyone will be very happy. But heaven isn't a place up in the sky. It's a time when people live with God in a life that Jesus rules.

Are there really golden gates in heaven?

The Bible refers to gates of heaven in several places. In describing heaven as the city of God, the book called Revelation says, "It has a great high wall with twelve gates and with twelve angels in charge of the gates" (Revelation 21:12). These gates are sometimes thought of as being pure gold, but the Bible describes them as being made of pearls. That's why some songs call the gates of heaven the "pearly gates." But of course they really aren't gold or pearl gates because heaven is not a place with metal gates. The gold or pearl gates are just word pictures of how beautiful the entrance into heaven is.

What are the heavenly mansions?

Jesus said, "In My Father's house are many mansions" (John 14:2). He was calling God His Father and the place where God lives His Father's house. In God's house there are wonderful apartments and rooms for all the people who want to live with God. That's what Jesus meant by "many mansions."

Will I go to heaven if I'm good?

A person doesn't get into heaven or start living with God in heaven just by being good and doing good things. In fact, Jesus said that some of the worst people may get into heaven more easily than those who think they are good. (You can find that statement in Matthew 21:28-31.) Only perfect people—saints—can have a perfect life with God in heaven. So you couldn't ever be good enough to get into heaven by what you do. The Good News Jesus taught was that all people could become saints and children of God through God's forgiving all their sins. He's willing to do this for Jesus.

How can I be sure to get into heaven?

To get into heaven, a person needs God's forgiveness of all sins. You can have this by believing that God wants you to have it. And you can be sure He does. Jesus showed that. He even allowed Himself to be crucified so you could be sure that God loves you. You can't ask for any better proof than that.

When I die, will I become a ghost?

You are a person with a spirit before you die, and you will continue to be that same person after you die. When you die, your spirit will continue to live either with God or apart from God. But your spirit will be the spirit of the person you are.

Why does God let people die?

If we were all perfect and completely like God, there'd be nothing wrong and we would live forever. But we're not perfect, and neither is anyone else. So everything on earth must die sooner or later. After all, you wouldn't want to keep on living in this world forever, would you? God has planned a better life ahead for his children.

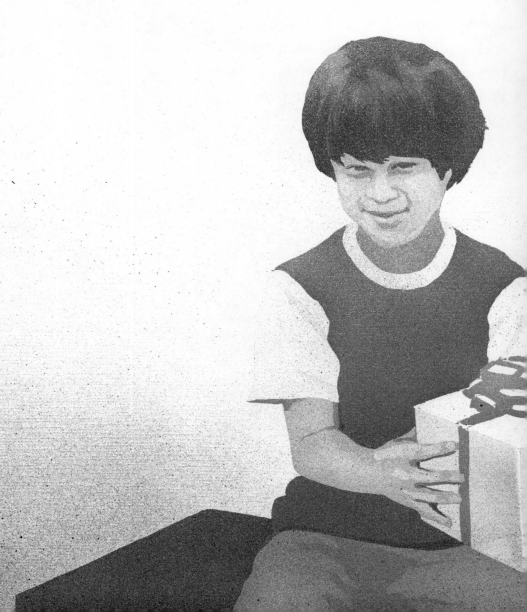

Do people know each other in heaven?

Oh yes. When Christians die, said Jesus, they continue to live with God in heaven. And they continue to live as persons. These persons can be recognized, as were Moses and Elijah when they once appeared with Jesus on a mountain. Those who know you will recognize you in heaven.

Do dogs and cats go to heaven?

Martin Luther once wrote a letter about heaven to his young son Hans. In it he described heaven as a lovely garden. In this garden there were also ponies for the children to ride.

The kingdom of heaven is wherever God rules, and this life with God can be enjoyed on earth. Dogs and cats also get to enjoy this life when their owners live with God. In fact, the Bible says that everything in nature wants this life. (Romans 8:21, 22)

Can people come back to life after they die?

Jesus once said, "I am the One who raises the dead and gives them life. Whoever believes in Me will live even if he dies. And whoever is living and believes in Me will never die." (John 11:26 HBFC)

So Christians believe that they will continue to live with God forever in heaven when they die. In that way they never really die.

My minister said, "Hell is where God isn't."
What does that mean?

The minister probably was saying that hell is not a single place. It's the life people have in being separated from God and not having God on their side. Sometimes the word hell means the kind of life people have after they die when they die apart from God and their Savior Jesus.

Is it possible to enter heaven without dying?

Since heaven is wherever God the Father and Jesus are, people enter the kingdom of heaven the moment they begin to live with God.

Once when Jesus was asked about the kingdom of God coming to people on earth, Jesus said, "The kingdom of God is among you" (Luke 17:21 RSV). He probably was referring to Himself and the life He was bringing to people.

Of course, heaven is also a life with God after death. That's why Jesus could say, "Whoever believes in Me will live even if he dies. And whoever is living and believes in Me will never die." (John 11:26 HBFC)

About This and That

Why do some people say, "God bless you,"
when I sneeze?

Sometimes we sneeze just to get rid of dust inside our nose. But we also sneeze when we're catching a cold. People who say "God bless you" when you sneeze are wishing you well. They are asking God to keep you from getting sick.

Will I live to be a grandmother?

Not if you're a boy. And even if you're a girl, only God knows how old you will get to be and whether or not you will have children and grandchildren. Those are blessings of God that not everyone receives.

What is the Passover?

It's a holiday celebrated every year mainly by Jews. It helps them remember how God saved the Hebrew people, their ancestors, from slavery in Egypt. The story is in the book of Exodus, chapters 11 and 12.

Why do Jews celebrate New Year's Day in the fall?

The calendar Jews used long before there were Christians has 12 months of 29 or 30 days each. Their year is only about 354 days. So every leap year they add a 13th month to make up the difference between their year and the 365 days other calendars have. The Jewish New Year is celebrated on the first day of the seventh month, which is usually September. This is a happy time in which Jewish people remember that God helped them go back to Jerusalem to rebuild the temple that their enemies had destroyed.

Why do people have to starve if God could feed them?

There is a saying that God has no hands but our hands to do His work. If all people would give money and food to the hungry the way God wants them to, no one would starve.

What's a miracle?

A miracle is a happening that is not according to usual laws of nature. It's a remarkable event because it differs from ordinary events and usually depends on the power of God. In the Bible miracles are special acts of God, such as Jesus healing blind Bartimaeus or Peter healing a crippled man at the entrance to the temple in Jerusalem.

Do miracles still happen?

A lot of doctors will tell you that miracles still happen often in hospitals. People who are expected to die suddenly begin to get well. People who pray a lot see miracles happen. What some people can't believe is possible becomes possible for those who pray and receive God's help.

What keeps the moon from falling?

The earth is like a magnet that pulls at the moon, but there are other planets that pull at the moon too. And there are forces that come from the sun and from the stars. Their pull is called gravity. It is gravity that keeps the moon on its course and keeps it from falling. The Bible says, "God has set the moon and stars in their places." (Psalms 8:3)

**Is it all right to give your body to science
or parts (transplants) to other people?**

There is nothing in the Bible that says you shouldn't. Anything people do for the good of others is an act of love, and that kind of loving is always all right.

Is it all right to burn a dead body?

Burning a dead body is called cremation. Some people, like the Hindus of India, cremate the bodies of dead people while others, like the Mohammedans, are against cremation. Most Christians prefer to bury the dead bodies of their relatives, but there is no law in the Bible that forbids cremation.

Why do people live in families?

Not all people live in families. Some live all alone—in apartments, in boarding houses, in college dormitories, in nursing homes. But most children live in a family until they become adults. Just imagine what your life would be like if you couldn't be a part of a family of some kind.

Is it all right for girls to look like boys?

When boys first started wearing their hair long, they often looked like girls, but that didn't make it wrong or right. It's all in what people get used to seeing or what style they prefer.

In the time when the Bible was written, men wore robes that were like dresses. Some Scotsmen still wear skirts. And in America lots of women now wear pants instead of skirts.

Styles change, but God really doesn't worry about appearances the way most people do. He's interested in what goes on inside your mind and heart. (1 Samuel 16:7)

Why do countries fight each other?

Most countries don't. Those that do fight a war either want something another country has or they are trying to protect and keep what they have. Some countries started a war because their leaders wanted more space for their people. Some leaders, like Hitler, wanted more power.

What makes clouds and rain and snow?

In the air there's a gas called water vapor. When warm air rises from the earth, the vapor cools and turns into tiny drops of water. These tiny drops join with very fine dust and make clouds.

When the water vapor in a cloud makes bigger and bigger drops, the cloud gets heavier and darker. When the drops become too heavy to stay in the air, they drop down as rain.

Jesus said, "God gives the rain" (Matthew 5:45). The same is true of snow, which is simply frosty rain. (Psalm 147:16)

Can people really see into the future?

Some things anybody can see ahead. For example, on a day when the sun is shining brightly we can be absolutely sure it will go down in the evening. Weather predictors aren't always right, but often they can see a storm coming days ahead of time. People who look far ahead into the future and try to see what may happen are usually just guessing. They're more often wrong than right in what they see.

Is gambling a sin?

Gambling to try to get money without earning it is a kind of coveting and selfishness. Selfishness and loving money is always foolish and wrong. It can lead to all kinds of troubles.

Why are church doors often painted red?

Red has many meanings for Christians. It represents, for example, the blood of Christ and the fires of the Holy Spirit. Through the years red has become a sign of the church. That's probably why the color is often used on church doors.

But there's no law that says what color a church door should be painted. Other colors such as green and white also have meanings, so you will see churches with their doors painted in colors other than red.

**In social studies we learned that there is supposed
to be a separation of church and state in our country.
What does that mean?**

There are different opinions on what that means. Some say the state, meaning the governments, should have no right whatever to tell churches what to do. They also believe that churches should not try to tell the government what to do.

Others think that the government ought to help churches because religion is an important part of the life of the people. They also think that church members, both separately and together, ought to help their government decide what is best for the people.

There are two points on which most Americans agree: that our government ought not favor one religion over another and that our government must never be allowed to *force* people to practice any kind of religion. That's called religious liberty. A separation of church and state for the sake of religious liberty is guaranteed by the First Amendment of the American Constitution.

**My sisters fasts once a week in order to lose weight.
She says fasting is commanded in the Bible. Is this true?**

Fasting is recommended in the Bible. At the time Jesus lived in Palestine, it was a Jewish religious custom to fast twice a week. When Jesus and His disciples were criticized for eating on a sabbath day, He said that His coming was a reason for celebrating rather than fasting. So fasting is not a law for Christians.

**All God's children are supposed to be free.
How free can I be?**

God's children are free from thinking they *have* to do or not do certain things to please God. They know that His love doesn't depend on what they do. But of course people who love God aren't *free* to do as they *please*; they don't want to *displease* God. So you can only be as free as love allows you to be.

**What do people mean when they say,
"The peace of the Lord,"
to each other in a church service?**

Ever since the time of Jesus some Christians have greeted each other or said good-bye with those words or something similar. "The Lord's peace" is a wish. It's wanting the other person to have the peace that Jesus gives to people—peace with God. By the way, Christians also used to kiss each other as they wished each other the peace of the Lord. A few still do. It's called the kiss of peace.